CONSENSUAL DISAGREEMENT
CANADA AND THE AMERICAS

Consensual Disagreement: Canada and the Americas aims at disseminating the Canadian dynamic and problematic to researchers and students interested in Canada and/or in inter or trans-American perspectives, and particularly to the participants of the International American Studies Association world congress [www.iasaweb.org] taking place for the first time in Canada, at the University of Ottawa, August 18-20, 2005.

The painting displayed on the cover is by the Canadian artist, Odette Imbert.
Title: *Tensions complémentaires.*
Private collection; Ottawa, 2002.

University of Ottawa
Research Chair:
Canada: Social and
Cultural Challenges in a
Knowledge-Based Society

Chaire de recherche de
l'Université d'Ottawa:
Canada: enjeux sociaux et
culturels dans une société
du savoir

CONSENSUAL DISAGREEMENT
CANADA AND THE AMERICAS

Edited by
Patrick Imbert

Université d'Ottawa
University of Ottawa

uOttawa

Library and Archives Canada Cataloguing in Publication

    Consensual Disagreement : Canada and the Americas / Patrick Imbert, editor.

Includes bibliographical references and index
ISBN 0-88927-277-8

    1. Multiculturalism – Canada. 2. Canada – Social policy. 3. Social psychology – Canada. 4. Globalization – Social aspects – Canada. 5. Globalization – Social aspects – America. I. Imbert, Patrick, 1948- II. University of Ottawa. Research Chair Canada: Social and Cultural Challenges in a Knowledge-Based Society

FC244.A4C66 2005   306'.0971   C2005-903078-X

For further information and for orders:
    http://www.canada.uottawa.ca/winwin
    pimbert@uottawa.ca

University of Ottawa Research Chair:
Canada: Social and Cultural Challenges in a Knowledge-Based Society (director: Patrick Imbert),

University of Ottawa, Département des Lettres françaises, 60 University St., Ottawa, Ontario, Canada, K1N 6N5.

Printed and bound in Canada

Contents

Introduction... 7
Patrick Imbert
University of Ottawa

Canada:
Three Centuries in the Americas................. 13
Patrick Imbert
University of Ottawa

Figures and Myths of Americas:
Blueprint for a Pragmatic Analysis.............. 51
Gérard Bouchard
Université du Québec à Chicoutimi

Canada on the Rocks!
Migrant Writing and Alterity 73
Daniel Castillo Durante
University of Ottawa

Index of Names.. 99

INTRODUCTION

Consensual Disagreement! This paradoxical expression may summarize the cultural dynamics that have led to Canada's perspective on multiculturalism and to its multifaceted role in the Americas. The strength which binds people who settled north of the United States and who contributed to the development of Canada while resisting its incorporation with its powerful and friendly neighbor south of the border, is probably based on the capacity to identify vectors of tensions and of contradictions, and to thrive on them. This is what **Gérard Bouchard** explores in his article dealing with the figures and myths of the Americas. As an intellectual deciphering socio-cultural dynamics in Québec and Canada, **Gérard Bouchard** aims at analyzing the ground on which one can establish relationships between the different regions of the Americas. Comparisons cannot be linked to common cultural features which would offer the pretext to invent a set of cultural elements common to the

Americas. However, they can be extracted from similar problems, deadlocks, and conundrums, expressed in a number of tensions and contradictions within the continent and in its relationship with former colonial powers.

At the epistemological level, this capacity to escape from an essentialist and dualistic vision attempting to mythically resolve contradictions, is an important feature of Canadian and Québec cultures in the context of the Americas and of globalization. The resilience that is displayed when facing contradictions allows an escape from craving for a master narrative which would exclude others and deny any validity to the expression of diversity.

Diversity, particularly when expressed by immigrants confronting the codes and norms of the new society giving them the means to express their potential, needs to be recognized. This diversity is emphasized by **Daniel Castillo Durante** in analyzing novels and essays published by Canadian and Québec writers born in Canada or in different countries of the Americas, such as Sergio Kokis, Dany Laferrière and Nancy Huston. In particular, **Daniel Castillo Durante** explores how stereotypes originating in the societies where the immigrants come from, confront those originating in Canada, notably the stereotype of the "Great North", if not of the "True North". The stereotypes are transforming as a result of the new context where they are applied. They eventually lead to the discovery of paths towards the establishment of temporary and practical ways of inventing peaceful social relationships oriented towards the future. This dynamic process leads to a consensual disagreement connecting the local and the global.

This particular expression of the encounter with the Americas within Canada takes place in a permanent transition in the midst of transnational cities such as Montréal and Toronto. They become laboratories for the invention of new solidarities and of a new conception of home. They are based more on shared democratic values than on territorial roots, a feature which has been explored by Manuel Castells emphasizing that "solidarity in a globalized world means global solidarity. And it also means inter-generational solidarity. Our planet is our only home, and we would not like the grandchildren of our grandchildren to be homeless".[1]

To have a home no longer means to be rooted permanently in a specific national territory defined by a homogeneous population. In our

---

1 Manuel Castells, *Information Technology, Globalization and Social Development*, Lausanne, United Nations Research Institute for Social Development, 1999, p. 13.

liberal democratic world, to have a home now means to share multi-faceted cultures combined to a set of fluid democratic values which can be carried along following the legitimacy and the necessity of geo-symbolic displacements. As it is demonstrated by the Canadian capacity to thrive on unresolved contradictions, to have a home also leads to the understanding that life is not a zero-sum game[2] and that, in a context of fostering change, there are numerous win-win situations.[3] It is in this context that **Patrick Imbert** presents the relationships between Canada, the Americas and globalization. **Patrick Imbert** emphasizes that Canada has demonstrated a remarkable capacity to safeguard the social protections of the Welfare-State while implementing policies rooted in an efficient economic liberalism open to free markets. As a result, Canada has mostly been able to connect what some people consider opposite tendencies, in an efficient active tension which allows for an original way to foster cultural, social and economic expansion.

---

2 Von Neumann, J. and Morgenstern, O., *Theory of Games and Economic Behaviour*. Princeton: Princeton University Press, 1944. See also: [www.canada.uottawa.ca/winwin].

3 Robert Axelrod, *The Evolution of Cooperation*, New York, Basic Books, 1984.

Putting together diverging tendencies can be directly connected to a dynamic adaptability which is an important feature of the changes brought forward by the liberalization of exchanges. This feature is also underscored by Néstor García Canclini in his book entitled *La Globalización imaginada* in which he studies the influence of globalization on Latin America: "To put it more clearly, what seems to be called globalization presents itself as a group of homogenizing processes, and a simultaneous process of fracturing, operating in a world that reorganizes differences and inequalities without eliminating them".[4]

In a nutshell, Canada within the Americas represents a good example of a culture based on a consensual disagreement linked to escaping the belief in life as a zero-sum game. These basic features contribute to the development of a socio-cultural and economic context adapted to the

---

4 Translation in English by P. Imbert. "Para decirlo más claro, lo que suele llamarse globalización se presenta conmo un conjunto de procesos de homogeneización y, a la vez, de fraccionamiento articulado del mundo, que reordenan las diferencias y las desigualdades sin suprimirlas." Néstor García Canclini, *La globalización imaginada*, Buenos Aires, Paidos, 1999, p. 49.

transformations brought about by the liberalization of exchanges, and to the renewed interest in the American continent expressed from within as well as from outside its shores.

Canada:
Three Centuries in the Americas

Patrick Imbert

University of Ottawa
University of Ottawa Research Chair
Canada: Social and Cultural Challenges
in a Knowledge-Based Society

Summary

In the 19th century, Canada, and particularly French Canada, dreamt of becoming an independent country. We will show that while there are numerous references to the independent countries of Latin America among Canadian thinkers as well as to Canada among some Latin American thinkers, the main attraction was provided by the USA, which was able to escape early from the grips of Europe, economically, technologically and culturally. However, slowly but surely, Canada became an independent and influential force on the continent notably through multiculturalism and the capacity to recognize difference while insisting on common basic principles of democratic life and on the promotion of civil society. Through its capacity to safeguard the social protections of the Welfare-State while implementing policies rooted in an efficient economic liberalism open to free markets, Canada's influence on the continent continues to grow, particularly in connection with the logic of globalization aiming at legitimizing geographic, social, cultural and economic mobility.

1. Self-Identification in the Americas: The Relationship to Europe

For many years, Canada, like many other countries of the Americas, turned an awestruck gaze towards Europe. The authorities of New France never approved of the epic tale of the *coureurs des bois* mixing with the indigenous peoples. This same epic was also displeasing to the ecclesiastic authorities, ideologically oriented in favor of Rome and the *Ancien Régime*, whereas the colonial office in London did its best to keep Canada within its bosom. In the years between 1870 and 1880, the Métis peoples of Manitoba suffered the consequences of this: they were marginalized and their chief Louis Riel was hung. This vision which rejected the large open spaces of the forest and of the prairies and viewed it as a barbaric place in need of civilization by the city, the town or the ideological garden, can be found in the Americas as a whole. This particular vision is expressed in the famous essay *Facundo*[1], by writer and president of the Argentinean Republic, Sarmiento, as well as in the concept of "frontier", where the creation of open spaces leads to the elimination of the native populations. In a way, Canada, a British colony, shares with the independent countries of the Americas not a culture, but an imaginary that is anchored in the barbarism/civilization[2] binary opposition that finds in immensity, dangerous places that must be transformed by a sedentary lifestyle and most of all, by the right to property[3] as it is emphasized in all democratic countries.

During the 19th century, Canada manifests its presence in the Americas by imaginary perspectives, which match those of the continent

---

1 Domingo Faustino Sarmiento, *Facundo*, Barcelona, Planeta, 1986.

2 See Patrick Imbert, "Barbarie/civilisation dans les Amériques au XIXe siècle: les espaces imaginaires", in *Exploring Canadian Identities/vers l'exploration des identités canadiennes* (E. Welnic, A. Branach-Kallas, J. Wojcik, eds.), Torun, Wydawnictwo Uniwersytetu Mikolaja Kopernika, 2002, p. 111-31.

3 Hernando de Soto, *The Other Path: The Invisible Revolution in the Third World*, New York, Harper and Row, 1990.

constructed by conflictive yet influential relations with Europe. In effect, at this time the intellectuals of the Americas are inspired by the Enlightenment (Rousseau, Voltaire), by Romanticism (Lamennais, Saint-Simon, Lamartine), and by economic and/or social theoreticians (Victor Cousin, Adam Smith, John Locke, Jean-Baptiste Say). Simultaneously, the same intellectuals drew attention to the European powers attempting to reconquer the territories of the Americas as did Napoleon III in Mexico.[4] The shared imaginary perspectives were founded on a disequilibrium that sharpened, as Gérard Bouchard[5] highlights, a sentiment of inferiority, a traumatism associated with leaving Europe behind and a problematic linked to alterity.

In this context, Canada is remarkable because of its democratic political system, its capacity to

---

4 Divergences are strong between Francisco Bilbao opposing Napoleon (*El Evangelio Americano y páginas selectas*, Barcelona, Maucci, 1920), and the collaboration of French-Canadian Faucher de Saint-Maurice who supports the occupation of Mexico by French troops (*Deux ans au Mexique*, Montréal, Cadieux et Derome, 1875).

5 Gérard Bouchard, "Sur l'analyse des figures et mythes des Amériques", Colloque *Mythes et figures littéraires des Amériques*, p. 3, Montréal, UQAM, May 2004. See also the research project directed by Zila Bernd: [www.sociocritique.mcgill.ca/mythamerique.htm].

combine dependence to Great Britain and its dream of independence. More recently, Canada has been recognized for its capacity to disseminate its technological, scientific and economic endeavors, its cultures and particularly its recognition of alterities through multiculturalism and bilingualism. These dynamics make it an important partner in the new relationships established through the multiple free exchange agreements between countries of the Americas in the context of globalization.

2. Aiming for Independence

In Canada, from the point of view of a potential rupture with Europe and its colonial relationship with England,[6] we can see the importance of the

---

6 "Pouvais-je oublier que j'appartenais à un peuple qui a le triste avantage d'être une exception sur le continent américain où la liberté politique a pénétré partout excepté au Canada? Pouvais-je oublier que j'appartenais à un peuple qui n'a pas le droit de se donner le titre de nation et qui n'a pas la force de le prendre?" (Louis-Antoine Dessaulles, *Six lectures sur l'annexion du Canada aux États-Unis*, 1851, Montréal, Gendron, p. 47). Could I forget that I belong to a people who has the sad advantage to be an exception on the American continent where political freedom has penetrated everywhere except in Canada? Could I forget that I belong to a people

right to happiness that is inscribed in the Constitution of the United States. This interest can also be found in the suggestions made by R. E. Caron who disseminates the *Manifeste adressé au peuple du Canada par le Comité constitutionnel, de la réforme et du progrès* on the 5th of November 1847: "Notre mémoire sera responsable envers notre postérité de la somme de bonheur plus ou moins grande que nous lui aurons légué".[7] The happiness evoked by Caron is linked to the importance given to commerce, industrialization, invention, diffusion of knowledge, and principles such as the personal growth of the individual and of his or her liberty, rationalism and equality of rights, and the right to property. These principles lead certain individuals with conflicting interests to those of England, to diffuse in 1849 the *Manifeste d'annexion* asking for annexation to the United States. Even if this endeavor does not lead to political changes, the culture of

---

who does not have the right to claim the title of natio-nand who does not have the strength to wring it? Our translation.

7 R. E. Caron, *Manifeste adressé au peuple du Canada par le Comité constitutionnel de la réforme et du progrès*, Montréal, Fréchette, 1847, p. 25. (Translation by the author: Our (collective) memory will be responsible towards our posterity of the greater or smaller sum of happiness that we will have left for her in heritage).

progress is disseminated in Lower Canada (Québec) by l'Institut canadien. In Upper Canada (Ontario), this culture is built in the public school system designed by Egerton Ryerson who is inspired by Horace Mann of Massachusetts who also influenced Sarmiento in Argentina.[8] In French Canada, despite Mondclet,[9] who wants schools to produce Canadians with a culture similar to the one developed by the Republic of the South,[10] the *ultramontain* French

---

8 He speaks of this culture in *North and South America: A Discourse Delivered Before the Rhodes Island Historical Society* (Dec, 27, 1865) (*Obras*, XXIX, 86) (book review in the *New York Herald*) as well as in the review entitled *Ambas Américas* that began publishing in New York in 1865.

9 Charles Mondelet, *Lettres sur l'éducation élémentaire et pratique*, Montréal, J.J. Williams, 1841.

10 This tradition is prolonged into the 20th century most notably in *L'homme qui va* by Jean-Charles Harvey where it is announced that the North American Republic will extend from the North Pole to the Panama Canal. This is very similar to Sarmiento's ideas: "I do not mean to make providence an accomplice in all America's forward movement since at another time this theory might be used to justify attempts at attracting politically or uniting with (or "annexing" as the American say) Canada, Mexico, etc. If that day comes, the union of free men will begin at the North Pole and for lack of further land, end at the Istmus of Panama."

Canadian clergy allied with England, and led by the bishop of Montréal Monseigneur Bourget, disseminates a nationalism inscribed not in the international market, but in a Catholic universalism, which has similarities with Ecuador's[11] and its dictator García Moreno. Étienne Parent's[12] economic liberalism that aims for rapid economic development of countries, and whose similarities with Sarmiento's line of thinking are remarkable, had to make due with this discourse, and vice versa. As such, Canada is a particularly unique case because of its position as a British colony protecting a traditionalist catholic ideology, and where forward thinking democratic parliamentarism also flourishes.

British parliamentarism also inspires thinkers in Venezuela, Cuba and Argentina. Coupled with British capital, it offers a different approach from the American republican-capitalist model linked to Manifest Destiny and to the United States dreams of being the Entrepôt between Asia and

---

(M. A. Rockland, *Sarmiento's Travels in the United-States in 1847,* p.123).

11 See: A. Berthe, *García Moreno: Président de l'Équateur, vengeur et martyr du droit chrétien: 1821-1875,* Paris, Retaux Bray, 1892.

12 Étienne Parent, *Discours prononcé par E. Parent devant l'Institut canadien, 19 novembre 1846.*

Europe as explained in *The American Register* of 1817: "If the influence of the mercantile spirit were excluded from the examination and decision of questions of this sort (the Americans must of necessity, by reason of their situation, become the Entrepôt of Europe and Asia), it would soon be conceded that there is no nation which has not a direct interest in promoting the natural growth of the resources of all others. It is from the great colony established in America by Europeans that Europe will learn this important lesson".[13]

3. The Americas and Canada during the 19th century

On July 23, 1840, Upper Canada unites with Lower Canada. However, Canada, the new country, owes one million dollars to the Baring Bank of London. Like in other countries, for example in Latin America, banks partly control the future of the nations of the Americas.[14] They are controlled by British directors and English capital,

---

13 *The Conspiracy of Arnold and Sir H. Clinton against the United States and against General Washington reprinted from* The American Register, New York, Arno Press, 1972, p. 7.

14 Note that under Napoleon III, France doesn't hesitate to invade Mexico because Mexico can't repay its debts.

from the Bank of Montreal to the Banco Nacional of Buenos Aires in the southern part of the continent. But Canada is already, in part, favored by the British presence because the dependence on the British Empire will lead Canadian banks to prosper during the 1930's in a number of Latin American countries. Moreover, Canada exports engineers to Latin America to help construct the rail system bringing to mind William Perkins of Toronto who develops the city of Rosario's infrastructure plan and designs the railway between Rosario and Buenos Aires.[15] Above and beyond their differences, connections exist between the Americas during the 19th century: Canada does more than export catholic missionaries or nuns to Chili or to Oregon. The tradition based on exporting technological know-how leads us to the important contemporary presence of Canadian multinational companies[16] that have offices in

---

15 Silvia Docola, *William Perkins: un Canadiense proyectando ciudad/region: Rosario 1858/1874,* in *Les discours du Nouveau Monde au XIXe siècle au Canada français et en Amérique latine/Los discursos del Nuevo Mundo en el siglo XIX en el Canadá francófono y en América latina,* (M. Couillard and P. Imbert, eds.) Ottawa, Legas, 1995.

16 Alcan, Bombardier, Cascade, Le Cirque du Soleil, etc., are well known Canadian multinational companies.

many countries in the Americas and around the world. In particular, one can think of engineering companies such as SNC Lavalin and information technology companies such as CGI.

Latin America and a continental conscience is also present amongst intellectuals like Papineau: "In common with the diverse nations of North and South America that have adopted the principles outlined in this Declaration...".[17] This conscience is also present in a text written by the Venezuelan thinker Fermin Toro who cites a section of the Declaration of Independence of Lower Canada written by the Patriots of 1837 in French Canada. However, Fermin Toro took his information from the British *Times* dated the 7th of December 1838: "From now on, Lower Canada is free of all obedience to Great Britain."[18] He uses this text to affirm that only independence can lead to economic progress. He then adds to his Constitutional project that the individual must be able to choose his or her country of resi-

---

17 "Adresse de la Confédération des Six Comtés au Peuple du Canada" (1837), in *Papineau* by F. Ouellet, p. 80.

18 Our translation of the phrase quoted from: *Europa y América*, in *La doctrina conservadora*, Caracas, Ediciones commemorativas del sesquicentenario de la independencia, 1960 (1st éd. 1839), p. 35. This phrase represents a hasty interpretation of the failed revolt of the Patriots.

dence.[19] Another thinker, Mathias Carvalho from Brasil is also interested in texts that indicate that many Canadians would like to sever the colonial link. In 1886 he publishes *Poemas americanos*, a translation of poems by Louis Riel, the métis leader who wanted to create a métis country in the Western part of Canada.[20]

4. Affirmation Comes With Success

Fermin Toro's ideas regarding the democratization of displacement, previously exclusive to the rich and noble, lead us to better understand what causes the world to dream about the Americas. Such displacement also aims for social mobility[21]

---

19 This theme is developped in Patrick Imbert, *Trajectoires culturelles transaméricaines*, Ottawa, Presses de l'Université d'Ottawa, 2004.

20 Mathias Carvalho, *Louis Riel: poèmes Amériquains* (Jean Morisset ed.), Trois-Pistoles (Québec), Éditions Trois-Pistoles, 1997.

21 This is well noted by numerous intellectuals. For example, Murat: "Croyez vous que j'irai demander à quelque farceur de me *classer*, quand je suis sûr de conquérir par moi-même la place quelconque à laquelle j'ai droit dans l'échelle des êtres?", A. Murat, *Esquisse morale et politique des États-Unis de l'Amérique du Nord*, Paris, Crochard, 1832, p. 358. (Do you believe that I will ask any person to categorize me in a class when I am certain

as demonstrated by Sarmiento. He contests the essentialist nature of attribution in 1847 in his journal that he kept during his voyage to Canada and to the United States: "The Yankee is a born proprietor... he does not say that he is poor but that he is poor right now."[22] The rejection of a static attribution is connected with the capacity of the United States to foster democratization at all levels, a notion initially evoked by Tocqueville, one that nowadays, includes the democratization of consumption, education and private access to information.

In the postmodern liberal contemporary context, this legitimization of displacement is even more a part of the culture of people in Canada, the United States, and in many countries of Latin America. It is expressed in novels such as *On the Road* by Jack Kerouac or *Volkswagen Blues* by Jacques Poulin. This same legitimization can also be found in contemporary literary and media discourse transforming the concept of *maison* or *casa*, whose meaning is now closer to the concept of home, that is, of a transportable set of values

---

to wring by myself the place I have the right to get in the hierarchy of beings?) Our translation.

22 Michael Aaron Rockland, *Sarmiento's Travels in the United States in 1847*, Princeton, Princeton University Press, 1970.

which are not necessarily rooted in a specific territory as can be seen in the film entitled *Home* by the Montréal filmmaker Phyllis Katrapani.[23] In this evolution, there is a desire for an expansion that is no longer geographic; rather an engagement that began with the development of industrialization, and that now subsumes cultural creativity and knowledge-based societal synergies as well as their practical and social applications.

5. Canadian Cultures and Their Continental and Global Diffusion

As it has already been seen in the barbarism/civilization binary opposition, cultural content is often linked to the permanence of certain stereotypes[24] like that of the belief in life as a zero-sum game,[25] where some win and the others lose. This concept can be seen in modern clichés where cul-

---

23 *La Presse*, Mardi 27 août 2002, p. C3. See also Patrick Imbert, "Globalization and Difference: Displacement, Culture and Homeland", in *Globalizations,* vol. 1, no. 2, December 2004, p. 194-204.

24 For a theory of stereotyping in the context of alterity, see: Daniel Castillo Durante, *Les dépouilles de l'altérité*, Montréal, XYZ, 2004.

25 For the belief in life as a zero-sum game, see: [www .canada.uottawa.ca/winwin].

ture is framed by the frontiers of the Nation-state. Canadians think: "On est né pour un petit pain" or "You can't win". More and more, these clichés make way for the new frontier defined as the exploration of the knowledge-based society where the new stereotype is based on the belief that life is not a zero-sum game. Therefore, it is possible to create new wealth without automatically wringing wealth from somebody else. Such a dynamic was emphasized in 1981 by Marcel Baril, the President of the Chamber of Commerce of the Province of Québec and one of the founder of the Mercuriades.[26] In this context, the "identity" is not linked only to a territory but also to the capacity to explore diverse images of the self. It is clearly highlighted by Pico Iyer in *The Global Soul*: "In that respect, Toronto felt entirely on my wavelength. It assembled many of the pasts that I knew, from Asia and America and Europe; yet unlike such outposts of empire… it offered the prospect of uniting all the fragments in a stained-glass whole".[27] The new situation allows for individuals to exert true influence on one another, in

---

26 *Les Affaires*, printemps 2005, édition spéciale *Les Affaires*: "25 ans de Mercuriades: 25 ans d'entrepreneurship au Québec", p. 7.

27 Pico Iyer, *The Global Soul*, New York, Vintage, 2000, p. 125.

the sense implied by Geertz,[28] that is to say, in a Canadian and democratic way, thanks to a "consensual disagreement" that feeds off of constant negotiation.

The possibility of escaping the stereotypical belief of life as a zero-sum game[29] is particularly poignant for the francophone elite whose bilingualism allows to contextualize itself in more than one culture. The necessity to be bilingual recently turned into an advantage as a result of the policies of the Trudeau Government favoring bilingualism at the Federal level as well as the impact of globalization and of the growing presence of other voices in the liberalization of exchanges. In effect, within the context of globalization and inter-American relations, bilingual francophones are able to escape the *not quite* of Bhabha[30] for whom to know more (one's own maternal lan-

---

28 Clifford Geertz, *Local Knowledge: Further Essays in Interpretive Anthropology*, New York, Basic Books, 1983.

29 See: [www.inter-disciplinary.net/ci/interculturalism/ic2/ic04cfp. htm] P. Imbert, "The Belief in Life as a "Zero-sum Game" and the Belief in Life as a "Win-win Game" and Intercultural Relationships." in *Interculturalism: Exploring Critical Issues*.

30 Homi Bhabha, "Of Mimicry and Man: The Ambivalence of Colonial Discourse", *October,* 1984, no. 28, p. 125-33.

guage as well as the dominant language) led to the exclusion from power networks. Now, bilingual Franco-Canadians avoid the stereotype of life as a zero-sum game (to speak French is either to lack integration into the Anglophone community, or to lose French through assimilation) as can be seen in a recent advertisement paid for by the Cité collégiale that reads: "FRENCH speaking students BILINGUAL employees".[31]

In Canada, official[32] and practical bilingualism is often coupled with multiculturalism. Certain individuals consider this situation threatening to the necessary sense of unification needed for social struggle, mobilization and protection of social acquisitions: "Multicultural Policies, critics worry, erode interpersonal trust, social solidarity and political coalitions that sustain the Welfare State."[33] However, as Keith Banting and Will Kymlicka suggest, the supposed solidarity may

---

31 *Ottawa Business Journal*, April 24, 2000, p. 11.

32 There are different kinds of bilingual education in the Americas. In Latin America, Paraguay is officially and practically bilingual (Guarani/Spanish), but Chile and Peru, among others, are also legally promoting bilingual education, at least for indigenous peoples.

33 Keith Banting, Will Kymlicka, *Do Multiculturalism Policies Erode the Welfare State?*, School of Policy Studies, Queen's University, Kingston, Ontario, Canada, Working Paper 33, August 2003, p. 2.

have never existed. This point of view would be shared by many thinkers in Latin America. For instance, Luis Enrique López[34] emphasizes that if indigenous populations have had to become intercultural, this was not the case for métis (Mexico) or non-métis (Argentina) hegemonic groups, who monopolized the national category for themselves and excluded natives. The argument that multicultural policies could break solidarities depends "on the belief that life is a zero-sum game and that there is a fixed and static amount of time, energy and money that will be spent on political mobilization, such that any effort spent on one issue necessarily detracts from another."[35] In the context of the multiplication of exchanges between countries of the Americas, and particularly in light of the redefinition at work for creating new less asymmetrical relationships between marginalized and dominant groups, a critical evaluation of the concepts of multiculturalism and inter-culturalism is in progress. If multiculturalism can be seen as a descriptive notion,

---

34 Luiz Enrique López, "Trece claves para entender la interculturalidad en la educación latinoamericana" in Mario Samaniego y Carmen Gloria Garbarini (compiladores) *Rostros y fronteras de la identidad*, Universidad Católica de Temuco, Chile, 2004, p. 261.

35 Keith Banting, Will Kymlicka, p. 8.

inter-culturalism leads to a new social construction, which calls for the disappearance of the belief of life as a zero-sum game. In the context of the spread of liberalism, this belief is put into question in many regions of the Americas, and particularly in Canada. As such, through its multicultural policies that are not based in the United States' tradition of the melting-pot, but on the capacity to enrich the rooted cultures by new elements from without, Canada, in its practices, is in the process of displacing this counterproductive belief in life as a zero-sum game. This is even more evident when one sees that the conception of multiculturalism in Canada leads to understand that culture and economy are linked, and that exclusion can be situated on a cultural and/or economic level. As a source of practical[36] multiculturalism[37] open to historically marginalized

---

36 See however the criticism made by Neil Bissoondath, *Selling Illusions*, Toronto, Penguin, 1994.

37 A textual legitimacy fostering a constant dialogue among citizens and their representatives, and open to redefinitions is therefore put in action and sets an example for many countries particularly in the Americas although it may be different in Europe as it is emphasized by Kymlicka. Considering Eastern Europe, he thinks that the Canadian model of multiculturalism may not be implemented in these countries. In effect, in

communities, Canada contests the stereotype of life as a zero-sum game. Hence, thanks to the dissemination of epistemological solutions as well as legal and practical realizations, Canada is able to participate in trans-American social and cultural redefinitions. They deal with the recognition that the Americas are places where different languages and cultures are present and can thrive, an important basis for the promotion of multiple aspects of civil society.

6. Canada's Influence in the Americas

The promotion of civil society can be seen throughout the continent through numerous examples. "Canada which held the Chair of the Committee on summit Management and Civil Society Participation in the Organization of the American States Activities until June 2003 has been very active in the OAS of which Canada became a member in 1989 under the government

---

these countries, minorities are seen as having collaborated with the enemies, the Turks in Bulgaria during the Ottoman Empire; the Hungarians with the Nazis in Romania. Consequently, the majority perceives multiculturalism as an internal threat. The weight of the warlike and genocide-ridden history is there and it recontextualizes the forward moving multicultural dynamic of Canada and the Americas.

of Brian Mulroney, and which has been under pressure from Canada… and other countries that recognized the utility and necessity of civil society participation."[38] Canada is also present in Haïti thanks to the Canadian International Development Agency's commitment to give it $147 million over the course of two years. We can also reflect on relations between Mercosur and Canada, to which Prime Minister Paul Martin "agreed to negotiate enhanced market access in the areas of goods, services and investment in the context of the creation of a future Free Trade Area of the Americas."[39] In the context of the important power differential[40] between Canada and the United States, multilateralism is seen as way to enhance the cultural and economic position of Canada. It has recently merged with a continental perspective taking as an example the success of banks and Canadian insurance companies in Latin America. However, this continental perspective is strongly linked to the benefits achieved by the North American Free Trade Agreement

---

38 Laurie Cole, *The Summit of the Americas Follow-Up Series*, Ottawa, FOCAL ed., no. 2, June 2003, p. 8.

39 FOCAL POINT: *Spotlight on the Americas*, January 2005, vol. 4, no. 1, p. 6.

40 In year 2000, Canada's Gross Domestic Product was about 10 percent of the GDP of North America.

(NAFTA). These benefits lead Daniel Schwaben[41] to propose an agenda that would build a more tightly-knit community in North America, a move that would enable Canada and its NAFTA partners to link more efficiently with Latin America and the Caribbean. These links are even more important considering that the European Union has once again become Euro-centric. The immense importance of the United-States in North-America and in the world, and the relatively low presence of Canada in Europe leads H. Klepak to conclude that "Latin America emerges as the only true avenue for diversifying our international relations, whether they be economic, political or cultural."[42] This analysis of the situation indirectly connects Canada to the myth of David and Goliath and could be applied to Canada's and Québec's cultural vitality in particular. The capacity of Québec's téléromans to compete against Hollywood products in English Canada[43] and to penetrate markets is well known.

---

41 See Daniel Schwaben, "Au-delà de l'ALENA – Faire une communauté de Nord-Américains", [www.ledevoir .com/2005/03/23/77619.html].

42 Hal P. Klepak, *What's in it for us? Canada's relationship with Latin America*, The Focal Papers, Ottawa, 1994, p. 13.

43 Gisele Tchoungui, "The Québec Téléroman: Between the Latino and the Wasp, a TV Serial with Gallic Humor in North America", *Québec Studies*, vol. 25, Spring 1998, p. 3-22.

One thinks of the production of Guy A. Lepage and his team entitled *Un gars, une fille,* which has been successfully featured in France, Greece, Poland, Spain, etc. One reason for the success of these productions is their capacity to differentiate from the canonic productions stemming from Brazil, Venezuela or the United States by their humor and original mix of fiction, reality and virtuality, while being cross-fertilized by the genre. However, in many domains, there is room for expansion particularly when one considers that Canadian exports to Latin America amount to less than one percent of Canada's total number. One could also add that Canada could take more from the diversity and wealth of cultural productions created for instance in Argentina, Brazil, Cuba, Mexico or Peru. One has to think of the popularity of tango, of the incredible number of musical productions exported from the Caribbean and Latin America, of a successful collaborative Argentinean-Canadian film such as "El lado oscuro del corazón",[44] and of many collaborative literary projects as outlined in two issues of *ellipse.*[45]

---

44 The production is by Eliseo Subiela and Roger Frappier.

45 *ellipse* 73: *Argentina-Canada* (Guest editor: Hugh Hazelton), Winter-Hiver 2004-05. *ellipse* 74: *Canada-Argentina* (Guest editor: Patrick Imbert), Spring-Summer 2005.

Canada is far from being limited by its national borders. It is a country that exports itself in different ways. This is very different from the 1970s when artists and intellectuals complained that they had a very restricted public and that Canadian productions were locked in small localities. Apart form Céline Dion and films featured by Denys Arcand, a telling example is Le Cirque du Soleil and its very high quality trans-cultural performances, which has been able to establish a highly mediated presence in the global centre for media-based entertainment that is Las Vegas.[46] In a nutshell, through its capacity to blend cultural differences in daily social relationships, Canada understands how to share its knowledge with others.

7. Thriving on Tension

One should also emphasize that even in the global context of the trimming of the Welfare State, Canada has been able, more than most countries, for instance Argentina,[47] to maintain some of its

---

46 This success was started by a group of individuals from the Charlevois county in Québec. It can also be linked to the success of The novel *Life of Pi* published by the Montréal writer born in a Francophone family, Yann Martel who received the most important literary prize in the Anglophone world, the Booker Prize.

47 Adriana Rizzo, "Crise économique argentine: Médias, 'les autres' externes et internes" in *L'interculturel et l'éco-*

social programs while subscribing to the cultural and economic creativity of free-trade and liberalism. Best-selling Canadian author Don Tapscott speaks to this particular topic in *Creating Value in the Network Economy*[48] in which he discusses the new created wealth stemming from a knowledge-based generation and from an adaptability to change that adds itself to social protections. However, Gilles Paquet underscores the relatively poor performance of Canada in Research and Development, and the slow progress achieved in creating modular and neural-net-type innovation systems, which would foster better economic and socio-cultural productivity and help "local systems of innovation to emerge and to fit into global networks". This relationship between the local, the national and the global is also examined from a social and cultural perspective by Néstor García Canclini[49] in the context of the relationships

---

nomie à l'œuvre (D. Castillo Durante and P. Imbert, eds.), The Americas Series, vol. 3, Ottawa, Éd. David, 2004, p. 73-95.

48 Don Tapscott, *Creating Value in the Network Economy*, New York, Harvard Business Review Book, 1998. He is widely quoted in business dailies and magazines in Latin-America along with Alvin Toffler and *Future Shock*.

49 Néstor García Canclini, *La Globalización Imaginada*, Buenos Aires, Paidós, 1999.

between Mexico and Latin America with the USA and Canada. Both Paquet and Canclini suggest that contemporary knowledge-based societies need to reconfigure concepts of identity in order to engage in economic and cultural investments open to taking more risks and to inventing a "strategic State" displacing "the current mythology built around the creation of "national systems of innovation".[50]

It is through a social-democrat thinking combined with a liberal economist aim that the Canadian cultures reread the culture of the self made man,[51] which is disseminated over the con-

---

50 Gilles Paquet, "Productivity and Innovation in Canada: A Case of Governance Failure", *Policy Options*, March-April 2005, p. 42.

51 See the comments of one of Sergio Kokis' character in *Le Pavillon des miroirs*, Montréal, XYZ, 1999. This character admires his father who attempts to spread the use of technology to the residents of his brazilian town: "Mon père sait un tas d'histoires de ce genre, qui se passent en Amérique du Nord et qui parlent de pauvres ouvriers très courageux: ils inventent des choses modernes et deviennent patrons parce qu'ils savent l'anglais. Papa croit beaucoup aux inventions; il est sûr qu'un jour il va devenir riche comme les Américains." p. 79. (My father knows a lot of such stories, which take place in North-America and which feature poor and very courageous workers: they invent modern objects and become bosses because they know English. Dad believes a lot in

tinent by the United States. Canada allows for the dissemination of multiple discourses in competition through the Multiculturalism Act of 1988,[52] the Employment Equity Act of 1986 and the Canadian Charter of Rights and Freedoms of 1982. These innovations dealing as much with social policy as with competitiveness and technological innovation contribute to differentiating Canada from the culture of the self-made man, the frontier and Manifest Destiny. They contribute to creating a continental divide between Canada and the United States as it is defined by Seymour Martin Lipset.

The difference in cultural dynamic can be seen in the recent legitimization of marriage for gay and lesbian couples in Canada. It is because of this influence that the Knights of Columbus of the United States have sent some two million cards to churches in Canada so that people can express their disagreement to politicians. The Canadian example is believed to be dangerous for

---

inventions; he is sure that one day, he is going to become rich like the Americans). Our translation. See also: Robert Stinson, "S.S. McClure's *My Autobiography*. The Progressive as Self-Made Man", *American Quaterly*, Vol. 22, no. 2, Part 1, Summer 1970, p. 203-12.

52 Multiculturalism can be defined as fostering diversity through shared values and institutions.

the culture of the United States as this legislation necessitates a reconfiguration of traditional concepts: marriage has come to be known as the legal contract between two persons and not a religious bond between a man and a woman. This displaces the traditional anti-nature concept that underlies the homosexual/heterosexual opposition, no longer synonymous with the barbarism/civilization binary and its corollary: exclusion.[53]

8. Being Canadian and Wanting America

As proclaimed by an immigrant character in *Cette grenade dans la main du jeune nègre est-elle une arme ou un fruit*[54] written by Dany Laferrière, a Montréal writer originally from Haïti, Canadians dream of America as a whole, that is to say that they dream of achieving promises of expansion, liberty, and future happiness. This sometimes happens by reconnecting one's self to the territory such as the case of Nunavut where the Inuits, who represent the majority, now decide their own

---

53 See: *Exclusions/Inclusions* (D. Castillo Durante, A. Colin, P. Imbert, eds.), The Americas Series/ Collection des Amériques/Collección de las Américas, vol. 4, Ottawa, University of Ottawa/Legas, 2005, 270 p.

54 Montréal, VLB éditeur, 1986.

futures. This example of political, economic and legal suppleness has been noted in native[55] communities of the Americas who have access to information about the changing status of natives in Canada through the Internet. This tool puts them in direct contact with the Government of Canada, one of the most technologically oriented governments in the world for its public access to an enormous amount of documentation and information online.

The capacity to foster social protection (free health care/social programs) as well as economic growth coming from an economic liberalism realized through the North-American Free Trade Agreement connects well with the identity of the Francophone Québec population who is able to link to a continental americaness without leaning towards Americanization.[56] In fact, Quebeckers who strongly consider themselves as belonging to

---

55 Concerning the indigenous problematic, see: *Futures and Identities: Aboriginal Peoples in Canada/Avenirs et identités: les peuples autochtones au Canada* (Michael Behiels, ed.), Canadian Issues/Thèmes canadiens, vol. XXI, Association for Canadian Studies, Montréal, 1999.

56 Frédéric Lesemann, "L'Américanité des Québécois passé par un rôle actif de l'État-providence", *Québec Studies*, Vol. 29, Spring-summer 2000, p. 43-53.

a continental territory such as North-America (in contradistinction with those who limit their range to a more local territory such as the Province of Québec) also consider themselves more different from the people living in the USA than the Quebeckers who do not identify themselves as being part of North-America. They are inclined to recognize that Québec has a different cultural identity than "American" culture[57] because it can put together diverging tendencies. The capacity to combine social and economic aspirations is also underscored by Jennifer Welsh[58] who studied the behavior of the Nexus generation (young people born in the 60s and 70s) in Canada and in the USA. She discovered a convergence of cultural behaviors except for those pertaining to religion and government, and particularly in the role of the Welfare State. However, this discovery is contested by other researchers who shared their views during the 105th American Assembly: "Canada and the United States share the most fundamen-

---

57 Léon Bernier et Guy Bédard, "Américanité-américanisation des Québécois: quelques éclairages empiriques", *Québec Studies*, Vol. 29, Spring-Summer 2000, p. 22.

58 Jennifer M. Welsh, "Is a North-American Generation Emerging?" *Canadian Journal of Policy Research*, 1.1., 2000, p. 86-92.

tal values rather than disagree about them"[59] such as a belief in freedom, freedom from fear, the free market, democracy and equal opportunity. Hence, instead of concentrating on values, one has to study the "perception of differences in values", which has had an impact on the Canada-United States relationship in the past few years. This comment should also be connected to the one underscoring that there are more differences within Canada and within the United States than between the two countries. This awareness could contribute to transforming controversial disagreements between Canada and the USA into consensual ones.

The capacity to escape from the belief in life as a zero-sum game, and to put together different aspirations, is contextualized with Canada's links with the United States, Europe and international bodies such as the UN, the commonwealth, NATO, the G-7, NORAD, NAFTA and the Francophonie. All of these partnerships prove that Canada is an influential partner at the continental level. As was mentioned at the Fifth Forum of Hemispheric Experts[60] in June 2004, Latin

---

59 *Renewing the US-Canada Relationship*, New York, The American Assembly, 2005, p. 4. See [www.americanas sembly.org].

60 *Northstar V Report*, FOCAL, Ottawa, 2004.

America and the Caribbeans are becoming increasingly heterogeneous. Hence, Canada with its tradition of multiculturalism and its capacity to put together economic liberalism, security,[61] and social welfare is particularly apt to shun from a "one size fits all" policy as it is emphasized in the *Northstar V Report*. The Minister of Foreign Affairs, Pierre Pettigrew recently underscored at a meeting of the conference entitled "Canada and the World",[62] that Canada is perceived as a reliable partner able to pursue efficient policies in a context of difference and divergence. This can lead to consolidating democracy, as well as to connecting business interests with local and sectorial developments goals and elaborating a collaborative approach to regional security.

---

61 However, Daniel Drache underlines the fact that "no public legal assessment of the impact of homeland security on Canada's Charter of Rights and Freedoms has been released…" See *Borders Matter: Homeland Security and the Search for North America*, Black Point, Nova Scotia, Fernwood, 2004, p. 4.

62 The conference was organized by the Institute for Canadian Studies at McGill University in collaboration with the Centre d'étude et de recherche internationale: [www.cerium.ca/article797.html].

9. New Borders and Canada's Global Expansion

Similarly to other countries, notably the United States who, from an object of national study became an object of international study, as it was noted by Sheila Hones and Julia Leyda,[63] and who, from a continental territory, became a hemispheric territory says Djelal Kadir,[64] Canada is not restricted by geo-political borders. Canada is therefore the object of international and trans-American studies. Canada's expansion is most noticeable because of its cultural, technological, mineral and industrial exports, impact in the resolution of global conflicts, its desire to help, its financial networks, and because of the importance and excellence of its 300 Canadian studies centers based within and outside of its national borders.[65] Thousands of Canadian and non-

---

63 See for American Studies: Sheila Hones and Julia Leyda, "Geographies of American Studies", November 2004 (unpublished paper) [Hones@ask.c.u-tkyo.ac.jp] and [juleyda@yahoo.com].

64 Djelal Kadir, "Defending America Against its Devotees", [www.iasaweb.org].

65 See for example the results of external research: "Las aportaciones sociales de Canadá en las Organización de Estados Americanos", "Maria Guadalupe Canchola

Canadian specialists connect their knowledge of Canada and its cultural, legal, economic and political dynamic with knowledge of their own countries and disseminate their comparative perspective to thousands of students. Take for example the specialized centers on law and bijuralism (La Plata: Argentina), on the literature of Québec (Porto Alegre: Brazil), on the economy (Mazatlan: Mexico), as well as all the centers in the United States, Paraguay, Venezuela, etc, that promote the capitalization of knowledge about Canada. These centers are based on the promotion of intercultural relationships, and the democratic rights of the individual working to improving society's function through shared mutuality and inter-transferable values.[66] They also help to disseminate the typically Canadian practice of consensual disagreement, which helps foster an ongoing dialog

---

Camacho" (theses), Universidad Nacional Autonoma de Mexico, 2004. For more information see: [www.iccs-ciec.ca].

66 This connects with "the Brazilian paradigm of enhanced progressive labour creativeness, and the Argentinean evolved federative social compassion." See Roque Callage Neto, "Between the Empiricism and the Unlimited Dream, America's Search for Transcendental Self-Determination", (*Interamerican Essay*, Universidade de Brasilia: rcallage@unb.br), p. 9 (to be published).

linked to the future, and they lead to a definition of what is acceptable and what is not acceptable in the context of a democratic society when dealing with other cultures.

Conclusion

The goal of a liberal cultural approach such as it is expressed in Canada, is to develop the individual semiotic faculty of populations, so that they might establish original links with different elements and units, and invent contexts in tune with cultural differences. The goal is to achieve a society in which each and every citizen will turn his/her hermeneutic capacity toward progress and consider that heritage rather comes from what has been planned for the future than what is transcended from the past. By progress we mean the capacity to foster citizenship more than territorial identity, and to validate the difference of the other while fostering individual development and protecting any individual from what is destructive and intolerable for a liberal democratic culture to which most immigrants, and particularly women born in authoritarian cultures, strive for. This is a dynamic that culturally complements the new links established between the economies of the countries within the Americas, and the new challenges imposed by the emphasis on homeland security in the United States. These links and challenges help reconfigure the strategic ambivalence of Canada in its foreign relations and to reframe its own self dynamic definition as it is manifested through consensual disagreement. These links and challenges represent a step toward a "renewed confederation of complementary opportunities linked to multidimensional democracies",[67] something that had been dreamt up by Lincoln in the USA, Sarmiento in Argentina, Vargas in Brazil and Trudeau in Canada.

Biographical Note

Patrick Imbert, born 1948, (Ph. D, University of Ottawa, 1974) is a Full Professor at the University of Ottawa (Department of French), University Research Chair Holder: "Canada: Social and Cultural Challenges in a Knowledge-Based Society", Executive director of the International American Studies Association, co-founder of the City for the Cultures of Peace and Fellow of the Royal Society of Canada. He has published 16 books. Nine books deal specifically with Canada and/or the Americas. *Roman québécois contemporain et clichés* (1983), *L'Objectivité de la presse* (1989), *Les discours du Nouveau Monde au XIXe*

---

67 See Roque Callage Neto, Ibid., p. 10.

siècle au Canada français et en Amérique latine/Los discursos del Nuevo Mundo en el siglo XIX en el Canadá francófono y en América latina, (with Marie Couillard) (1995), *The Permanent Transition* (1998), *Trajectoires culturelles transaméricaines* (2004). Among the collaborative books, 3 are published in the Colección de las Américas/ The Americas Series/Collection des Amériques: *L'interculturel au cœur des Amériques* (with D. Castillo Durante) (vol. 2), *L'interculturel et l'économie à l'œuvre/Interculturality and Economy: The Margins of Globalization* (with D. Castillo Durante) (vol. 3), *Exclusions/Inclusions: Déplacements économico-symboliques et perspectives Américaines/Discourses of Exclusion and Inclusion: Economic and Symbolic Displacements in the Americas* (with D. Castillo Durante and Amy Colin) (vol. 4).

Mailing address:	University of Ottawa, 60 University St., Ottawa, Ontario, Canada, K1N 6N5
Email:	pimbert@uottawa.ca
Tel. (office):	(613) 562-5800, ext.: 1092
Fax:	(613) 562-5981
Web site of the chair:	www.canada.uottawa.ca/winwin

FIGURES AND MYTHS OF AMERICAS BLUEPRINT FOR A PRAGMATIC ANALYSIS

Gérard Bouchard
Université du Québec à Chicoutimi
Canada Research Chair on Collective Imaginary

Summary

This paper outlines an approach able to support various research projects and, more particularly, the construction of a dictionary of figures and myths of the Americas, to which the author is a contributor.[1] The paper is also written as part of a research program on collective imaginaries dealing with Québec, Canada, and the Americas (Canada Research Chair). Accordingly, it deals with the discursive practices, the representations (or symbolic configurations) that they produce, and their social grounding. A double level of analysis is advocated, one focusing on figures and

---

1 This project, which regroups numerous contributors, is underway, under the direction of Prof. Zila Bernd at Porto Alegre, Brazil (Universidad Federal do Rio Grande do Sul-UFRGS). See: [www.sociocritique.mcgill.ca/mythamerique.htm].

metafigures, the other on myths and archemyths. In keeping with the proposed definitions of these concepts, the collective symbolic configurations are considered as the outcomes of discursive strategies, as mediating devices intended to overcome contradictions. Various examples are offered in order to illuminate these theoretical and methodological outlooks.

Warning: In its present version, the paper discusses the figures and myths promoted by descendants of Europeans in the Americas. The figures and myths specific to the indigenous people will be addressed elsewhere.

1. An Analytical Framework

1.1. First Option

Among the various pathways available to analyze the figures and myths of Québec, Canada and the whole American continent, two broad orientations can be identified. According to the first, one assumes the existence of a common culture, a "pan-Americanity" of the first degree which manifests itself through similar traits in the three Americas. If so, the task of the researcher would consist in building a repertory of these traits – that is: the major known figures and myths (I will come back to these concepts). This option, however, seems to me quite risky for various reasons, namely the fragility of its postulate.

A number of propositions have been set forth in order to characterize the skeleton of this hypothesized pan-American culture. I recall five of them, which are the most common and the most appealing: a) Latinity, b) métissage, miscegenation, c) uprootedness, transience), d) baroque (impurity, delinquency, transgression), e) hybridity, trans-culture. Yet, I think that, while each of these threads connects with important dimensions of the cultural life in the Americas, none of them covers the entire landscape, far from that.

I will restrict myself to a few brief remarks. Very obviously, the Latinity criterion excludes major parts of the Americas (Indians, Blacks, all British-descent citizens, Germans, Asians, etc). Moreover, Latinity represents only part of the whole process of cross-breeding. Actually, métissage does not run very deep in the history of societies like Québec, English Canada, United States, Haiti, Argentina, Bolivia, Southern Brazil and the likes. Likewise, uprootedness and "migrancy" are only one face of the population dynamics of the Americas. The other face, as prominent, tells a very different story of settlement, rooting, community formation and integration, fear and rejection of the foreigner, reproduction of traditions and identities, resistance to external, ethnic inputs. As to hybridity and trans-culture, they must not occult a long history of forced assimilation, destruction of cultures – if not, flatly, of populations. Finally, baroque has often flourished along with its contrary: attempts to replicate the superior ("classical") cultures of Europe, to implement an ethics of faithfulness and imitation of the Old World, an attitude which dampened creativity and invention. The widespread concern for a "pure race" reflects the same spirit of monolithism.

If there is no such thing as a pan-American culture, a repertory-type approach might be ill-advised for a dictionary project. The resulting instrument would contain a large number of local or regional figures and myths, thus hurting the pertinence of the project. Another difficulty would come from the potentially unlimited scope of the data collection, in absence of a workable criterion to restrict it. In addition, a huge number of unrelated entries would limit the usefulness of the dictionary. Hence, all these remarks bring out the interest of an analytical approach.

1.2. Second Option

According to this second option, researchers, rather than assuming the existence of a common culture, should consider that all the cultures and nations[2] of the New World have been faced, at the outset and all along their history, with a similar set of problems, deadlocks, conundrums, expressed in a number of tensions and contradictions. In search of solutions to these common obstacles, each of them has devised its own discursive schemas, symbolic arrangements, taking the forms of figures and myths. And it comes that, among these figures and myths, one can detect similarities and differences – the latter being as interesting and instructive as the former.

In this direction, the first task is to identify these common axes of tension and contradiction (conflicting interests, incompatible ideals or principles, mutually exclusive requirements, unworkable compromises...). I offer a few examples that I have come across in my own research (of course, this is not an exhaustive list):

- To counter a feeling of inferiority, a lasting inhibition inspired by the prestigious culture ("civilization") of the mother country, as opposed to the perceived lousy, mediocre culture of the

---

2 I use the word "nation" since this was the concept retained by the New World elites to designate their collectivity. It is also through this notion that they have attempted to build their future as well as their past.

new nation (referring to this painful mindset, some Australian intellectuals talk about a "cultural cringe").

- To foster a strong distinct identity, while preserving the heritage of the mother country (language, religion, institutions). In other words: to fabricate Self-ness from Otherness.

- To enjoy the security of the cultural continuity with the European past but, at the same time, to endure with the impoverishing dependency that comes with it.

- To overcome the trauma associated with the break-up which, sooner or later, occurs (through a brutal event, or a piecemeal, incremental process) in the relationship with the mother country. Everywhere, indeed, this fracture is experienced, in various degrees, both as a much desired and welcomed emancipation, and an iconoclastic gesture, a betrayal.

- To manage the painful discrepancy between a) the sophisticated, distinguished culture of the elites, drawing on European contents and models, and b) the rugged culture of the popular classes immersed in the wild life of the new continent.

- To provide the new nation with a symbolic density, a moral authority of which she is deprived by virtue of being new, that is: improvised, artificial and lacking credibility. This is achieved by resorting to a collection of myths which emphasize the glorious origins, the great founding heroes, the magnificent accomplishments, the unique qualities, and the historical mission of the nation. Most of those national myths also celebrate its purity, its superiority, and its universality.

- To fill the lack of a prestigious past by coming around an apparently insuperable contradiction for a new nation: to claim remote roots, to build a long memory from a short history.
- To assert oneself as a real nation, as a homogeneous and united entity, despite the ethnic diversity and the strong social cleavages that existed at the very beginnings of the new collectivities – the most striking element being the encounter with the indigenous people.
- To forcibly, often violently, appropriate a territory which was already appropriated by original occupants and, at the same time, pretend to embody a superior civilization abiding to legal rules.[3]

Again, those are only examples, but the list could be expanded. What matters from our perspective is that, for each of them, a large array of figures and myths have been set forth as mediat-

---

3 For more on this, see G. Bouchard (2000).

ing devices, among which it becomes possible to detect recurrent discursive strategies intended to remove, occult, or articulate the contradictions.

1.3. Options Available at the Practical Level of Analysis

At the practical level, two ways are open. First, the analysis can proceed upstream; starting from any particular figure or myth, one wonders what contradiction it is supposed to resolve, what node it is intended to untie. For instance, the myth of the mermaid in Brazil, a symbol of hybridity and metamorphosis, can be seen as a mediator of oppositions related to racial dichotomies.[4] The pervasive myths of a historical mission, of the elected people, are obviously devoted to substantiate the fledgling national ethos and to offset the uncertainty and fragility that comes with the "newness". And the powerful myths which emphasize the youth of the nation, its energy and creativity, are an efficient response to the void that follows the departure with the mother country's trajectory.

The analysis can also proceed downstream; starting with a contradiction, one looks for the ensuing figures and myths, like in a descending

---

4 Forthcoming paper by Licia Soares de Souza.

genealogies. For instance, in colonial Mexico, the Creoles were faced with the problem of implementing the national model (with its homogeneity premise) in a bi-racial society where the Whites felt much superior to the Indians. As a result, they were led to promote their fellow citizens by resorting to the myth of the lost tribe of Israel. This way, the Indians were made equals, partaking in the old Christian heritage. Likewise, the Creoles deeply resented (v.g. the "cultural cringe") the attacks by European intellectuals (Montesquieu, Humboldt, de Pauw, and others) who mocked their lack of history and patrimony. The indigenist myth, asserting the Indian ancestry of the Creoles, provided a solution to this problem: from then on, through a process of symbolic appropriation, the Creoles could claim and celebrate the Indian heritage as *theirs*.

As we see, this kind of approach also lends itself to a search of recurrences, and since the array of possible discursive inventions is not unlimited, it is possible to reconstitute a language, a grammar.

2. Definitions, Theoretical Insights

The preceding comments are based on particular assumptions which call for explanations. The approach advocates a foray into the field of collective imaginary defined as a body of symbolic landmarks through which a collectivity inscribes itself in space and time. Every imaginary involves the institution of five kinds of relationship:

- A relationship to space, through which a geographical unit is transformed into a territory, that is, a space which is inhabited, laboured, named, dreamed, narrated, in short: appropriated.
- A relationship to the social, through which every individual is assigned a rank or a status on a scale of wealth, prestige, and power.
- A relationship to Self and to Other which fuels an identity dynamics of inclusion/exclusion.
- A relationship to the past as expressed in a collective memory.
- A relationship to the future which generates utopias, dystopias, or any kind of anticipation.

It is worth noting that our definition of the collective imaginaries places the focus not on the discursive practices and their psychological determinants, but on their products (representations, myths, systems of thought...). For practical reasons, the analysis of their anchoring in the unconscious is not prioritized.[5]

---

5 For a more detailed account on this, see G. Bouchard (2003).

In the preceding pages, I have referred to the notions of figure and myth, to which should be added the notions of metafigure and archemyth. The word **figure** designates all kinds of representations or systems of representations likely to be disseminated and to take root in collective imaginary. The figure may be considered as a second degree symbol in that it is a group of symbols or an organizing key of symbols. It exerts a structuring effect among its components, which share a common denominator. The figure may express itself as a character or a status (bastard, victim, hero), a state of mind (emptiness, ambivalence, autonomy, alienation), a feeling (nostalgia, fear, joy), a situation, a condition (loneliness, poverty, marginality), acts, behaviours, events (betrayal, re-conquest, sacrifice, revenge), operations, processes (recycling, mixture, transgression), and forms (linearity, circle). In the course of a text, figures are not necessarily explicitly named; they can appear as fragments, being only suggested or vaguely delineated. Then, they must be detected through inference and interrelations among a set of symbols.

The figures are differently federated according to the type of discourse in which they originate. For instance, fiction (metaphor), argumentation (rhetoric), and empirical analysis (evidence) are three associative principles which intervene in various degrees according to the vector involved (literary text, sociological theory, political ideology, scientific monograph). However, regardless of the vector, figures remain major components of collective imaginaries wherein they are more or less closely articulated to each other: they may form a system, they may be loosely assembled, or simply juxtaposed; they may also contradict each other, etc.

The **metafigure** is a collection of related figures, variants of a common motif. Metafigure operates with figure the same way the latter operates with symbols. Here are a few examples of metafigures drawn from the Québec contemporary literary corpus:

- É. Nardout-Lafarge (2001) has demonstrated that the theme of waste, scraps, remains, combined with a discourse of disenchantment and parody, is the matrix of Réjean Ducharme's writings.
- According to M. Biron (2000), in Jacques Ferron's novels, the metafigure (my word) lies in the celebration of freedom (the capacity to change, to reinvent one's life, to start anew). However, for G. Michaux (2001), the core thread is built around the theme of disarray, uncertainty, and incompletion.

- Analysing a group of novels by Michel Tremblay, A. Brochu (2002) has concluded that the moon was the overarching symbolic structure.
- The same author (1988) had previously established that several Gabrielle Roy's novels were driven by a quest of the inner personal truth, the hidden quintessential in the depth of the soul, where can be found the key of liberation.

   Altogether, the figure and the metafigure account for the form of a discourse, for the mechanical arrangement, the relational nexus of its components. Let's say that they belong to the morphology or the structure analysis. This is a first level. The notions of myth and archemyth belong to the second level. While it is symmetric, homologous to the former, the latter is the locus of the pragmatic analysis per se, where one wonders about the functions of the figures, their social and political concomitants or determinants, the strategy of which they are parts, their anchoring in a *praxis*. Here, the analysis deals not with figures and metafigures but with myths and archemyths. In this perspective, myth is a representation or a set of representations intended to implement, in a sustainable way, a meaning expressed in a value, a belief, an ideal. Thus, myth both promotes and "promises"[6] in order to serve a hidden agenda, to overcome a contradiction, or to escape an unfavourable course of action. It mediates symbolically a situation that cannot be handled in a rational way.[7] And it does so according to a logic of power struggle, persuasion, mobilization, and action. Admittedly, this definition is restrictive, it overlooks important dimensions of myth, but it fits the needs of the pragmatic analysis that I have chosen to pursue.[8] At the same time, it can be said very comprehensive since it encompasses various kinds of representations and meanings.[9]

6　Patrick Imbert, personal communication.

7　A good example at hand is the social mobility myth in the United Sates: the sharp socio-economic inequalities are pictured as temporary, treatable (not "structural"); everybody can change and is responsible for her/his condition and fate; everything is possible to any talented individual, providing the appropriate effort is made.

8　As we know, Lévi-Strauss also addresses myth as a mediating device in a situation of contradiction, in a quite different perspective. The analysis is carried out in the context of "primitive" societies and the mediation is said to operate unconsciously, through a ritual, rather than through explicit discursive strategies.

9　A typology is needed which would distinguish between several brands of myths: archaic, literary, scientific, identity…

In addition to that, the reader will note that I free the concept from four references typically given as structural or inescapable, which present the myth as a) a narration, b) an account of origins, c) a celebration of the sacred, d) an epic. To most scholars, these are universal characteristics of myth; I rather hold them as major traits which sometimes manifest themselves and sometimes don't. For instance, a number of great contemporary myths in the Western world are not narratives and do not refer to the origins nor to the supernatural. I also distance the concept from any evolutionist overtone. Indeed, I do not embrace the vision of the past which posits that, first, there was a supremacy of myth and then, progressively, reason took over. To this well known schema, I oppose the view that, basically, irrespective of the time period, any system of thought – or any system of representations – is a varying combination of reason and myth. I also assume that, while partly empirically grounded, it mostly belongs to fiction. As a result, myth cannot be assessed primarily on the basis of its truth but on the basis of its symbolic and social efficacy, on its capacity to support the never candid operations of reason.

This is in keeping with the pragmatic scant of the suggested approach: discursive strategies and their products are addressed as being, somehow, always related to classes, elites, social groups, occupational networks, communities *in situation*, facing threats, fears, involved in power struggles, projects of conquest, in all cases acting to protect or promote material, social, or symbolic interest.

The relation of archemyth to myth is similar to the relation of metafigure to figure: in both cases, we deal with a structuring configuration of kin components. The two levels (morphology and strategy) must be seen as complementary. They operate on the same material but in two different ways. The former comes first, it draws a preliminary chart, it brings to light relational groupings among a disordered list of figures. From there, the latter brings out the social articulations.

3. Four Metafigures/and Archemyths

In the course of my comparative research on the formation and transformation of national cultures in the New World, I have come across a number of figures/myths that I have been able to relate to metafigures/archemyths. In concluding, I offer four examples.

The great antinomy of civilization and barbarism. It has been expressed time and again through a set of familiar dichotomies (made up of figures and myths) such as: reason/superstition, culture (or civilization)/illiteracy, classicism/

baroque, center/periphery, modernity/tradition, European/Savage, rural/urban....[10] Whatever the variant considered, this configuration went (and still goes?) deep and wide in the discourse of the New World intellectuals who felt constantly challenged by this dual category.

The millenarist utopian cycle. This is a three-fold cycle which can be traced under various forms in the cultural past of most new nations. The initial step consists in great dreams and utopias typically associated with a Golden Age and echoing the enchantment of collective beginnings. Then this founding utopias fail, which fosters a sentiment of disenchantment, sullenness. The third step is the time of re-conquest, a willingness to reintegrate the lost paradise, repeated attempts to redress the broken equilibrium – hence a painful dialectics of dream, collective action, and failure at work at the regional scale as well as at the national level. One thinks, here, of the dream of the great Columbia in Latin America, the recovery of the lost sea in Bolivia, the recovery of the stolen northern territory in Mexico, the trauma of the Deportation in Acadia (Canada), the fracture of the 1760 Conquest in

10 The list is not exhaustive; see, for instance, F. Ainsa (1999).

the history of Québec, the quest for a separate province or state in Saguenay (Québec), a case that is the subject of my novel *Mistouk* (see also G. Bouchard, 1989), etc.

The dialectics of closure and opening. The history of a number of new collectivities shows a back-and-forth dynamic between introverted and extroverted attitudes and behaviours. It is particularly obvious in the case of the United States, always torn between, on the one hand, nativism, xenophobia, provincialism, isolationism (expressed in various ways all along their history, one of them being the Monroe Doctrine) and, on the other hand, open-mindedness, universalism, expansion-driven policies, imperialism. Likewise, the history of Québec is a puzzling mixture of psychological withdrawal, inward-looking moods, unassertive episodes (xenophobia, localism, past-oriented mentality, conservatism, ruralism) and opening, self-confidence, optimism, expansionism – for instance: the taste for exploration, the conquest of the North, the dream of a coast-to-coast Francophone nation, the strong sense of a continental (if not worldwide) mission, the massive emigration to the United States, etc.

The New World relay of civilization. This configuration has surfaced just about everywhere in the new nations. The basic idea is that, after the waning of ancient Greece and Roma, Europe was entrusted to pursue the task of civilization and it lamentably failed. Over the centuries, it became deeply corrupted and turned its back on its great historical mission. Yet, this betrayal can be remedied. Fortunately, indeed, the New World is there to take over, with its redeeming power and resources, material as well as moral (land, manpower, freshness, youth, belief…). Again, this archemyth has received many formulations, from the "cosmic race" in Mexico (Jose Vasconcelos) to the "American dream", or the project of a "small Athenian Republic" in Québec (Edmond de Nevers).

Again, what precedes is preliminary. This paper is only intended to outline the skeleton of an approach, a work in progress; many other examples or lines of investigation could be mentioned. Moreover, several representations pop up in the new nations' discourse, which do not exactly fit the definition of a figure or a myth (for instance: trickster, metamorphosis, chameleon…). They seem to intervene as operational devices, discursive tools, and perform a specific, different kind of mediation.

Conclusion

As we have seen, this analysis of collective imaginaries dealing with Québec, Canada and the Americas places the focus on the products of the discursive practices (myths, archemyths…). To most scholars, however, the field of collective imaginaries extends much further to include the study of the unconscious as it has been defined by Jungian perspectives. This direction of analysis leads to unpack complex dynamics and universal, immutable structures which underlie the production of representations and, arguably, account for the striking recurrences observed across cultures and time periods. It is worth noting that, in the perspective of the pragmatic analysis, this direction of research is somehow sidelined. Indeed, the goal of our analysis is to proceed downstream, to articulate the discursive productions to a particular social context, rather than looking upstream for their possible universal rooting.

Bibliography

Ainsa, Fernando, "The Antinomies of Latin American Discourses of Identity and Their Fictional Representation", in Amaryll Chanady (ed.), *Latin American Identity and Constructions of Difference*, Minneapolis/

London, University of Minnesota Press, p. 1-25, 1999.

Bouchard, Gérard, "Une Nouvelle-France entre le Saguenay et la Baie-James: Un essai de recommencement national au dix-neuvième siècle", *Canadian Historical Review*, Vol. LXX, no 4, (décembre/December), p. 473-95, 1989.

Bouchard, Gérard, *Genèse des nations et cultures du Nouveau Monde. Essai d'histoire comparée*, Montréal, Boréal, 503 pages, 2000.

Bouchard, Gérard, *Raison et contradiction. Le mythe au secours de la pensée*, Québec, Nota bene/Cefan, 130 pages, 2003.

Bouchard, Gérard, *Les deux chanoines. Contradiction et ambivalence dans la pensée de Lionel Groulx*, Montréal, Boréal, 313 pages, 2003b.

Biographical Note

Trained in sociology and history, Gérard Bouchard has spent over twenty years conducting empirical, multidisciplinary research in various fields of social and historical sciences. During the last decade, he has shifted his research priorities towards cultural studies (*Genèse des nations et cultures du Nouveau Monde*, 2000; *Les deux chanoines*, 2003; *Raison et contradiction*, 2003; *La Pensée impuissante*, 2004). He is now doing comparative research on the formation and transformations of collective imaginaries, within a Canada Research Chair which he holds since 2002. Author of several books, he has contributed 250 papers to scientific journals and collections of essays.

Mailing address:	Université du Québec à Chicoutimi, 555 boul. de l'Université, Chicoutimi (Québec) G7H 2B1
Email:	bouchard@uqac.ca
Tel. (office):	(418) 545-5517
Fax:	(418) 545-5518

Canada on the Rocks!
Migrant Writing and Alterity

Daniel Castillo Durante
University of Ottawa

Summary

Collectively considered as the "Great North", Canada has proven to be a screen onto which phantasms are projected. This projection takes place within a discursive process where alterity conforms to the stereotype, as it can also be seen in Argentina. An equivocal anthroponomy (the euro-centric noun "AMERICA" is the cornerstone of a topological modernity based on expropriation and exclusion) is first imposed then consented to, and strips Canada of its right to *Americanism* as it is reserved for the United States. So, does Canada really exist? Even if it's a country deformed by the stereotype of the "Great North", contemporary Canada is reconfigured, although with some difficulty, on a literary level. It is indeed from the literary space of migrant writing, with the contradictory and often multiple knowledges and flavours that it offers, that it is possible

to see how the petrified image of Canada is desta-
bilized and called into question.

1. A Stereotyped Canada

Canada, viewed from the outside, is above all a
cliché. Its geography and climate contribute a
great deal to this: too large to understand its complexity and nuances, too cold to live there without
fear of becoming… a snowman. In order to
depict Canada's immensity while still confronting
the rigor of its extreme seasons, nothing is more
useful than the stereotype. Contrary to popular
thought, this tendency to express Canada through
overused and ready-to-use images emanates as
much from inside as from outside its borders. The
Quebecois poet Gilles Vigneault didn't hold back
when he exclaimed that, "his country is not a
country, it's winter". Furthermore, the *Petit
Robert*, while making room for Canada in its cat-
alogue of proper nouns, declines its identity by
specifying that Canada is the "country of large
spaces and of snow".[1] In arriving here, even the
most inspired European concedes to the very
tempting, prefabricated metaphor:

---

1 *Le petit Robert: dictionnaire illustré des noms propres*, Paris,
  Le Robert, 1994, p. 2168.

Amérique tendue aux quatre clous des vents
[…]
Amérique d'angine peau de râpe cœur de givre
toi ma gerçure[2]

How can we explain that the depiction of Canada often passes through a vision that eliminates its nuances, complexities and most of all, its unique voices? It is in a poem by a famous French Canadian writer that the fascination for the common place, while quite condensed, can be found:

La neige nous met en rêve sur de vastes plaines,
sans traces ni couleur
Veille mon cœur, la neige nous met en selle
sur des coursiers d'écume
Sonne l'enfance couronnée, la neige nous sacre
en haute mer, plein songe, toutes voiles dehors
La neige nous met en magie, blancheur étale,
plumes gonflées où perce l'œil rouge de cet oiseau
Mon cœur; trait de feu sous des palmes de gel
file le sang qui s'émerveille[3]

---

2 Michel Van Schendel, *Poèmes de l'Amérique étrangère*, Montréal, L'Hexagone, 1958.

3 Anne Hébert, "Neige", *Mystère de la parole*, Paris, 1960.

Born in Sainte-Catherine-de-Fossambault (Portneuf), Anne Hébert may have left her native land for France, but her vision of Canada, as much in her poetry as in her novels, will always be determined by a network of *topoï* relating to a hostile, rough, elemental and violent geography. Furthermore, on a lyric level, Gaston Miron, whose work constitutes one of the most powerful poetry in Quebecois literature, often leans towards a representation of the country conform to the cliché:

> *Compagnon des Amériques*
> *Mon Québec ma terre amère ma terre amande*
> *ma patrie d'haleine dans la touffe des vents*
> *j'ai de toi la difficile et poignante présence*
> *avec une large blessure d'espace au front*
> *au-delà d'une vivante agonie de roseaux au visage*[4]

The break in the poetic work upheld by Heidegger[5] no longer operates simply when there is recourse to a stereotypical representation of the Being. The *Dasein* (Being-there) according to the

---

4 Gaston Miron, "Compagnon des Amériques", *L'Homme rapaillé*, Montréal, Presses de l'Université de Montréal, 1970.

5 Martin Heidegger, *Acheminement vers la parole*, Paris, Gallimard, 1976.

German phenomenologist relates back, in the latest analysis, to all that alters the subject's relationship to the world, that is to say to the land that he or she calls home. How does this geographical place deploy itself in the time of the Being? Where can Canada's "there" be found? A gaze likely to disdain discursive scoria surrounding Canadian alterity requires that the discursive annexation of Canada according to the "Great North" ideologeme, a so-called virgin space ideal for colonial conquests, be called into question. In Argentina, Sarmiento[6] does just this when he associates the open spaces of *la pampa* to a sort of no man's land inhabited by the "Bedouin" people who must be, according to Sarmiento, banished from the earth's surface.[7] Contrary to Sarmiento's ideological perspective,[8] we suggest that Canada

---

6 Domingo Faustino Sarmiento, *Facundo ou Civilisation et Barbarie dans les pampas argentines*, Paris, Éditions de l'Herne, 1990 (the original was written in Spanish; the author was exiled to Chile in 1850).

7 Daniel Castillo Durante, "L'ethnicité argentine ou le tain d'une identité d'emprunt: de l'Argentine de Sarmiento à l'Argent-Inn de Sabato", *La littérature et les abattoirs de la modernité*, Vervuert-Iberoamericana, Frankfurt-Madrid, 1995.

8 For comparisons between Canada and Argentina or Canada and Latin America, see: *Les discours du Nouveau Monde au Canada français et en Amérique latine au*

will benefit from the discovery of the timbres of its multiple voices through a nomadic gaze. Could migrant literature incarnate this type of gaze? Is it possible to find within current cultural practices symptoms of a non-stereotypical gaze towards Canada? What are the conditions needed for a non-stereotyping gaze towards Canada? How can such a vast and complex country, subject to frequent transformations, be depicted without reviving the underlying prefabricates that its name evokes? On the other hand, one shouldn't represent Canada by using only positive stereotypes. Both extremes must be refused in order to understand how Canada, in certain respects, removes itself from a non-petrified gaze; this is to say that, as a nation, it presents itself as a sort of screen on which the other can project his or her phantasms. Place-screen, phantasm machine, is Canada the space where desire can exist only if masked?

XIXᵉ siècle/Los discursos del Nuevo Mundo en el Canadá francófono y en América latina en el siglo XIX, [Marie Couillard et Patrick Imbert, eds.] Ottawa, Legas, 1995, 288 p. See also: "Las bases del sistema territorial nacional frente a lo global en las Américas"(avec A. Rizzo), *Revista Cronía*, Universidad Nacional de Río Cuarto (Argentina). Año 4, vol.4, Nro 2, 2001/2002, p. 1-18.

2. Migrant Writing and the Reconfiguration of Canada

In *L'amour du lointain*, Sergio Kokis asks himself if a country such as Canada can really exist.[9] An inevitable figure of the neo-Quebecois literary space, the writer and artist-painter has difficulty believing that he was able to escape the Brazilian nightmare so easily. In effect, Canada appeared to him as a utopia-cum-reality. The narrator of *L'amour du lointain* essentially reactivates, with a child-like gaze, his shock in the face of the enchanted place called Canada. Is it real or just a mirage? His migrant gaze, decidedly opposed to returning to his native land, a Brazil decimated by the growing wealth of the elite to the detriment of the rest of the population, has difficulty focusing on such a vast and unfathomable space. The bedazzlement of this migrant gaze and its difficulty in conceiving of a space open and inviting to a foreigner adrift, creates divisive lines between North and South America. The literary word of Kokis establishes a foundation for a cartography of the migrant imaginary. Because of his emotional baggage, Kokis encounters a practical problem: how does one imagine – without recourse to utopia – a place likely to welcome the disenchanted,

---

9 Sergio Kokis, *L'amour du lointain*, XYZ, Montréal, 2004.

the left for dead, the marginalized of the Americas, the millions of people condemned to failure from the very beginning? Is there a place where education, health care and work are available to everyone? With a master's of psychology in hand, Sergio Kokis (a character in the textual margins of his of autobiographical narrative) arrives in Montréal. The downtown of this Quebecois metropolis, with its arrogant architecture and cars fresh off the assembly line, convinces him that he has come to a land of pure riches. Here, it is the logic of contrast that underscores the perception of Canada. Whether this contrast be colored with melancholy (Kokis) or with frenzy and euphoria (Laferrière[10]), it is the author that determines the balance. From his very first novel, *Le pavillon des miroirs*, the character depicting the foreigner focuses his gaze according to the following memoir:

> [...] Les gens de l'endroit restent distants, dans leur monde, insérés quelque part dans une existence palpable; tandis que lui, il flotte. Après tout, c'est lui le déplacé, pas les autres. Ils ont l'air d'être bien à l'aise tels qu'ils sont, où ils sont. Ils ont de la matière, tandis

---

10 See for instance *Comment faire l'amour avec un Nègre sans se fatiguer*, Montréal, VLB éditeur, 1986.

que l'étranger n'a que mémoire et carence d'attaches. Et puis cette insécurité si grande, qui le fait sursauter durant la nuit au moindre cliquetis du chauffage.[11]

The figure of the foreigner in Kokis' work (contrary to the work of Dany Laferrière[12]) uncovers superficial playfulness that aims, in reality, to espouse the neutrality of the anonymous. It is a mask that allows foreigners to go unnoticed while still protecting themselves from the threats that hover on the horizon of all exile:

Je me revois à la sortie de l'aéroport, m'étonnant de la taille énorme des automobiles, de l'apparence moderne de cette grande ville où je pouvais enfin me perdre, passer inaperçu. Rien ne m'y attachait, aucun souvenir, aucune souffrance. L'étranger porte un masque

---

11 Sergio Kokis, *Le pavillon des miroirs*, XYZ, Montréal, 1994.

12 In fact, according to Dany Laferrière, the myth of the Americas as a country of cockneys to which it is imperative to find access through success renders it anonymous since it becomes a question of winning in the fight for recognition. This rather binary interpretation of the Americas underscores his novel entitled *Cette grenade dans la main du jeune Nègre est-elle une arme ou un fruit?*, Montréal, VLB éditeur, 1993.

d'apparence anodine pour être accepté, pour qu'on le laisse en paix. Il n'est pas sûr des autres, ni prêt à abandonner sa nature profonde. Il joue un jeu pour s'intégrer. Par l'orifice des orbites il essaie d'apprendre à son corps cette danse qu'il singe mais qu'il ne ressent pas. Tel un nègre sur une patinoire, je m'agitais, maladroit et déséquilibré, cherchant à ne pas être ridicule à leurs yeux. Rien que pour un certain temps, en attendant que les choses se tassent là-bas.[13]

Le pavillon des miroirs is that on which the equilibrium and reasoning of Kokis' writing depends, the *clef-de-voûte* of his work, the place from where exile is accomplished as a sensory laboratory for the immigrant. "There" takes the shape of a conglomeration of images that constitute his "past". Often in conflict, these images demand, on behalf of the foreigner, a strategic mimesis that effaces the impression of ambivalence in which the migrant artist lives. The figure of the anonymous-foreigner takes on a dual function: it allows for a circumstantial integration (purely strategic), while giving rise to the free expression of phantasms, archetypal images as

---

13 Sergio Kokis, op. cit., p. 45.

well as reveries capable of substituting themselves for the space and time in which the voice of the "other" operates. Canada becomes a sort of clay, easily molded by the projections of the national imaginary. The figure of the foreigner as created by Kokis avoids clichés because he refuses to accept the ready-to-use representations of the immigrants' *new* homeland, a place intent on sub-jugating the other to the preconceived images it upholds. In this sense, the politics of integration in most countries of the Western World in fact hide a political will to promote conformity, the identity of the Same. To exclusively reflect on his own image, the foreigner offers the mask of anonymity like a white cloth on which conformi-ty has no hold. "Tell me what you will; I'm else-where", seems to exclaim not without irony, Kokis' character. Foreigner everywhere, even in his native land, the character discovers he belongs nowhere whereupon he refuses to be imprisoned by the stereotype of his origins. The clichés of the carnival and the commonplaces of the *samba* only serve to accentuate his feeling of rejection. Added to this is the fact that the foreigner of *Le pavillon des miroirs* practices a figurative art whose tor-tured portraits do not coincide with the stereo-type of Brazil, the author's country of origin and where the novel takes place:

Tout gênait mes visiteurs. Je me sentais encore plus mal à l'aise de devoir expliquer les légendes ou les références historiques que personne ne connaissait, les citations de poèmes que personne n'avait lus. Leurs commentaires étaient déplacés, avec des silences lourds comme lorsque quelqu'un n'ose pas demander où sont les toilettes. Le pire, c'étaient les réflexions béates sur le malheur des pauvres gens, sur le tiers monde ou, lorsque trop angoissés, ils poussaient la bienséance jusqu'à suggérer des interprétations sauvages sur ma propre personne. Très pénible, en effet. Je ne sais pas vraiment quoi faire dans ces situations, quand je dois arrêter de parler, si je dois montrer d'autres tableaux, comment je devrais abréger la visite. Heureusement que les gens savent réagir, qu'ils sont mondains, jouant avec le regard et le corps pour changer de sujet, s'extasiant sur un objet quelconque de mon atelier pour dévier des tableaux. Ou alors sachant que je viens de là-bas, ils bifurquent sur le carnaval ou la samba.[14]

Because of this double exile, the figure of the foreigner escapes the ideologemes underlying the

---

14 Ibid., p. 47-8.

representations of the stereotype.[15] The character's paintings and the lack of eagerness to adhere to the petrified images of his new society make him neither assimilated nor cultured. He wants to conserve the neutrality of anonymity that allows him to avoid succumbing to the stereotype. The stereotype, in this case, indicates that which seeks to force the foreigner to conform to a ready-made image. Whether he likes it or not, the foreigner will never succeed in fully grieving over the loss of his homeland because even when said homeland is masked by a wild quest to become American, the return of the repressed confronts him with loss.[16] Attached to an intensity lacking presence, Kokis' character multiplies in an art studio (symbolic of the maternal cocoon, the place of all places) the stunned expression of characters that seem to be blind to the world that surrounds them. Enclosed in their bubble, tainted black with melancholy's bile, nothing seems to satisfy

---

15 See: Daniel Castillo Durante, "Le stéréotype à l'heure de tous ses masques", *Sont-ils bons? Sont-ils méchants? Usages des stéréotypes* (Christian Garaud, ed.), Champion, Paris, 2001, p. 73-82.

16 This scenario applies to the situation of the black man in *Cette grenade dans la main du jeune Nègre est-elle une arme ou un fruit?* by Dany Laferrière (Montréal, VLB éditeur, 1993).

their shock of being there. From here, we can better understand the incomprehension of visitors grappling to understand difficulties abroad. Kokis, spider of exile, knits webs in which there is only room for tortured bodies. In the centre of this massive web, shines a self-portrait of the artist, lone witness to a world falling into emptiness. His characters, similar to those of Beckett, are only waiting for the worst. Confronted with so many contorted faces gathered in bunches of despair, the spectator, helpless witness to an atmosphere on which planes a bitter, deathly breath, is overtaken with malaise. Is this the promised bride of the foreigner? Will his wedding night, infinitely delayed, uncover the affective autism in which the exile exists? This noticeable identity gap between birthplace, past and the "palpable world"[17] is the space-time in which the foreigner will inscribe the signs of his wandering. The unloved past (that of the south that pushed him into exile) hides a fracture in between him and his memory. How does he live with the unbearable memory of that which he became disinherited before even leaving Brazil? The studio presents itself then as a place where ghosts who maintain the desire of the migrant artist in suspense are exorcised; the ultimate recognition of

---

17 Sergio Kokis, op. cit., p. 360.

the foreigner is death. The foreigner of Kokis'
novel, by summoning death as radical alterity
reveals, at the same time, the impossible task that
awaits the uprooted subject when he fervently
attempts to represent his past. In this way, isn't
migrant literature simply the expression of a
posthumous parole?

3. Cultural Translation, Alterity, and Clichés

Nancy Huston, who emigrated to France many
years ago, seeks Canada in loss, yet tolerates a prefabricated vision of her native land:

> Le Nord, j'en viens. En français, chaque fois
> qu'on y fait allusion, on précise qu'il est
> grand. On l'affuble même, souvent, d'une let-
> tre majuscule. Personne ne dit, parlant de
> moi: elle vient du petit Nord. Toujours du
> grand. Sa grandeur compense, dans l'imagi-
> naire français, son vide. Il est immense mais
> ne contient rien. Des arpents de neige. Des
> millions d'hectares de glace. On admire sans
> bien savoir quoi en dire, ni comment vous
> interroger là-dessus. On sait qu'il y fait froid.
> ("Dieu! qu'il fait froid!" Trente ans après avoir
> quitté le Canada, je revendique le droit de
> prononcer cette phrase à Paris, et d'avoir froid
> à Paris, merde, sans qu'on me réplique à

chaque fois: "En tant que Canadienne, pourtant, vous devriez être habituée"… me renvoyant, sinon dans mon pays d'origine comme les pauvres sans-papiers, du moins à mes origines…) "Le Nord", c'est aussi une façon de parler. En fait, Calgary, ma ville natale, est situé [sic] à la même latitude peu ou prou que Paris, ma ville adoptive. Le Nord, c'est une image. Une image pour dire qu'il y fait froid, et qu'il n'y a personne.[18]

Is it possible to avoid the stereotypical nomenclature of "Great North" that encapsulates Canada in a screen of ice? Huston may well try to live, write and publish in Paris, but the "Great North" continues to weigh on her. She tries to convince us that she would have lost it, but the reader is no dupe: no matter where she goes, her image as "Canadian" will always be associated to this "Great North" that, she says, is full of emptiness. After leaving Canada, a feeling of guilt replaced the aborted attempt to grieve: "My country was the North, the Great North, the true north, strong and free. I betrayed it, and I lost it".[19]

---

18 Nancy Huston, *Nord perdu*, Arles, Actes Sud/Leméac, 1999, p. 13-4.

19 Ibid., p. 15.

Is it possible to betray an overused image that immobilizes you within an empty space? Without vitality, deprived of substance, this image remains effective because the foreigner refers to it when considering loss. The lost North, the Great North comes to represent LOSS when the foreigner takes stock of the years lived abroad. Is Canada then the cliché that allows us to identify the emptiness that inhabits us? By what curious alchemy does its name – instead of alluding to a specific place – come to designate the fracture that the so-called "Canadian" subject feels when he or she assumes their identity? This would explain why the essential for Nancy Huston resides in "that which can be translated".[20] Isn't radical alterity, that which cannot be translated and that makes no concessions because it is indeed impossible to translate, important? Nancy Huston's ideas on the topic of Canadian alterity come to a dead-end. Her notion of "translation" proves to be problematic in the sense that she privileges the stereotype that controls the repre-sentation of otherness. To translate otherness in this context would be to make it conform to the prefabricated images society holds of it. It is rather in the *untranslatable*, in that which sub-

---

20 Ibid., p. 90.

tracts itself from the stereotypical representation, that the power to *alter*[21] Canada into an evolving space-time that resists the euro-centric discourse of conformity probably exists. It is precisely because the complexity of Canada's many unique voices are untranslatable that we attribute clichés and prefabricated judgments to it.

In her analysis of the migrant writer, Régine Robin sees a society in three places: Canada, Québec and Montréal.[22] Here, there is a rupture with the image of the "Great North" leaving room for an imaginary coming from the four corners of the world. Is it necessary to fragment Canada if we wish to break the icy cliché that freezes this nation to the point where it is rendered "translatable" and therefore consumable? Yes, in the sense that Canada avoids a singular approach perspective. The "Great North" proves to be a prefabricated response to the euro-centric discourse that transforms Canada into a postcard image. Why must the question of Canadian identity always bog us down in the deadlock arising from the desire for recognition? The category of the translatable proposed by Nancy Huston, whether we

---

21 See: Daniel Castillo Durante, *Les dépouilles de l'altérité*, Montréal, XYZ, coll. "Documents", 2004.

22 Régine Robin, Postface, *La Québécoite*, Montréal, XYZ, 1993, p. 209.

accept it or not, is underscored by this logic. To make Canada "translatable" would mean making it conform to an image (that of the Great North, "the true north, strong and free") that the European imaginary creates on its behalf. The substantialization of cultures, languages and writings denounced by Régine Robin[23] alerts us to the threatening obstacles that arise as soon as we attempt to contain alterity under the pretext of defining it. This essentialization of Canada leads to an implicit attachment to an alterity that would be *true, strong* and *free*. The revival of the ideologeme of the "Great North" presupposes thus the existence of a people in harmony with the message they convey.

4. From a Geopolitical Stereotype to a Multicultural Cartography

For this reason, it is difficult to understand how immigrants and all the other disadvantaged peoples of History, having sought out Canada as a new home, could recognize each other. To define Canada according to a geographic characteristic draws attention to determinism that immediately hinders consideration of a multicultural, fractal, plurilinguistic, postmodern, contemporary

---

23 Ibid., p. 218.

Canada. The chameleon-like being of Canada, that is to say its capacity for changing skins according to the different cultures that cohabitate there, remains sealed as long as we are unable to let go of the native land – a fixed trap, immutable, ready to bring us back to order eternally. Constantly evolving, aware of the geographic, economic, social, cultural, linguistic and religious influences originating from extremely diverse origins, Canada seeks its identity in diversity, and dare we say, in various types of conflicts that the primate of consensus doesn't always dissolve. One of the qualities of *La Québécoite* by Régine Robin was its accent on the role of the worried and worrying gaze of the immigrant subject living in Montréal, one of the urban, cultural and demographic foundations of Québec and Canada at the same time. It must further be noted that when the "ethnic novel" of Régine Robin was published in 1983, the Quebecois society hadn't yet opened its mental frontiers to different phenomena linked to immigration, the Diaspora and exile. Nonetheless, *La Québécoite* gives way to a wandering that reminds us of the foreigner who, with time, can finally put a name to his or her ghetto:

> Partout des boucheries kascher, des synagogues, des maisons de prières et des congrégations. La bagelerie Van Horn, l'épicerie

Budapest et le marché Aviv. Puis ils longe-
raient Outremont, les belles maisons le long
du parc Pratt. Ce serait le silence. Le quartier
endormi redeviendrait populaire au-delà. Ils
prendraient par le nord remontant la rue
Saint-Laurent jusque chez eux. Ce serait une
très longue promenade prenant des allures de
bout du monde. Ils ne l'entreprendraient que
certaines nuits d'été, de ces nuits au vent
léger, accompagnées de senteurs de lilas à la
fin de juin ou de roses plus tard, des senteurs
des jardinets entourant les maisons. Ils ne se
sentiraient totalement eux-mêmes qu'en
marchant, en traversant les différents quar-
tiers. On quitte un ghetto pour un autre,
murmurerait-il ironiquement, chez les Juifs,
puis chez les Italiens, en passant par chez les
riches. Que des ghettos. Tu as remarqué?[24]

Montréal therefore becomes the centre of the
world for many immigrants who manage to settle
their multiple, various, contradictory and shat-
tered imaginaries in a city that, similar to *Le livre
de sable* by Borges,[25] never tires. There is an infi-
nite multiplication of ghettos that form a

---

24 Ibid., p. 190.

25 Jorge Luis Borges, *El libro de arena*, Buenos Aires,
Emecé Editores, 1975.

labyrinth of superimposed and juxtaposed col-
lages never actually penetrating one another. It is
because of this first cartography that authors like
Yann Martel[26] strategically represent the
"chameleon", and help him accumulate multiple
identities without having to betray any of them.
Patrick Imbert analyses, with great lucidity, the
underlying logic proper to the character-
chameleon when he affirms, "in the discourse on
Modernity, the chameleon is conceived of as
trickster because it is necessary to pledge alle-
giance to one discourse or to one culture".[27]
However, in a postmodern/postcolonial perspective, abstaining from choosing an identity does
not presuppose any betrayal, as is the case with
Nancy Huston, but rather the rejection of a binary logic that, in the context of Modernity, has
only exacerbated the stereotypical representation
of the other culture.[28]

Despite this, the all-important city accepts all
kinds of strategies of invasion and identitarian
poaching that result in the immigrant keeping his
multiple identities. This is the case of Émile

26 Yann Martel, *Self*, Toronto, Knopf, 1996.

27 Patrick Imbert, *Trajectoires culturelles transaméricaines*,
Ottawa, Presses de l'Université d'Ottawa, 2004, p. 35.

28 See P. Imbert, "Cartography, Dualism, and Identity"
[www.relazionarte.it].

Ollivier's character who in *La Brûlerie*,[29] invites us to follow his itinerary, and whose child-like gaze has lost its reference points. The Côte-des-Neiges district in Montréal, largely open to the smells, tastes and knowledge of men and women coming from elsewhere in the world, is presented to the reader as a place of incertitude, precarity and ambiguity, of the migrant adventure of Canadian soil:

> J'ai marché sur le chemin de la Côte-des-Neiges, j'ai marché dans les allées de son cimetière, j'ai marché sur des milliards d'os et de têtes de morts. Sur la Côte-des-Neiges, le monde réel avec ses voies lactées et ses soleils: rages, débauches, folies dont je sais tous les élans et tous les désastres. Migrant, si vous vous hasardez sur ce chemin d'un pas flâneur, d'un pas de flâneur traînant, vous franchirez une espèce de frontière morale et métaphysique. On ne vous considérera pas comme tout à fait Québécois: il paraît qu'il faut l'être de naissance. Du moins, l'on vous acceptera comme un être humain. Ici, nous, on nous appelle: minorités visibles, mais paradoxalement on a l'impression d'être des spectres, des

---

29 Émile Ollivier, *La Brûlerie*, Montréal, Boréal, 2004.

invisibles, tout juste après les nuages et le souffle du vent.[30]

The possibility for the migrant writer to appropriate the toponymy of his adopted neighborhood, and then to inscribe his own quest in it, says a great deal about the porous, permeable character of the city he calls home. To write Montréal is to be reborn there according to a transformation in return for which the foreigner (including those considered "visible minorities") adopts the mimetic nature of the chameleon. As the Quebecois for whom exile, a touchy subject indeed, is associated with the loss of their *francité* or "Frenchness" on the American continent,[31] the foreigner – during his difficult quest, redraws the

---

30 Ibid., p. 15-6.

31 "Even though it emphasizes their minority status, the Québécois's inability to recreate on the American continent all of their lost *francité* [or "Frenchness"] is paradoxically their salvation. For this failure leaves open the original sore which enables them to recognize the other, to be the other. *Francité*'s incompletion makes it possible to *become other*, an element present in all culture and its true foundation", Fulvio Caccia, "L'Altra Riva", *Vice Versa*, Montréal, 1986 (quoted by Winfried Siemerling, *The New North American Studies: Culture, writing and the politics of re/cognition*, London-New York, Routledge, 2005, p. 130).

Canadian space to the point where he deceives the stereotype that wishes him to be as white as fleece.

Conclusion

Does Canada exist? In fact, it is the responsibility of each culture that inhabits this country to respond accordingly. The famous Canadian mosaic is conditional upon this. An elastic space in permanent negotiation, Canada demands extreme epistemological flexibility without which the gaze becomes strained and alterity is petrified. How is it possible to stay one's self while remaining open to difference? Is the motto ("Je sème à tout vent") contained in the *Petit Larousse Illustré* Canada's sole ambition? Obliged to reinvent itself each day to avoid transforming into a pit of historical phantasms, will Canada manage to free itself of the stereotype? Will Canada succeed in ridding itself of the geo-colonial myth that imprisons it in a block of ice? Will Canada escape from been always served on the rocks?

Biographical Note

Daniel Castillo Durante is the author of *Du stéréotype à la littérature* (prix Victor-Barbeau de l'Académie des lettres du Québec 1995), *Ernesto Sábato ou les abattoirs de la modernité, Sade ou l'ombre des Lumières*, *Les foires du Pacifique* (roman: prix littéraire *Le Droit* 1999), *Les dépotoirs de la postmodernité: société, culture et littérature en Amérique latine* and *Les dépouilles de l'altérité*. All of these works highlight the obstacles that threaten the precarious nature of artistic expression, notably literary, in societies devoted to immediate profitability. Professor at the University of Ottawa, Daniel Castillo Durante has published articles about literary theory and cultural critique in Argentina, Canada, France, Germany, Holland, Mexico, Peru, Puerto Rico, Spain, and the United States.

Mailing address:	University of Ottawa,
	60 University St., Ottawa, Ontario,
	Canada, K1N 6N5
Email:	dcastild@uottawa.ca
Tel. (office):	(613) 562-5800, ext.: 1098
Fax:	(613) 562-5981

Index

A

Ainsa, Fernando, 67, 70
Alcan, 22
Arcand, Denys, 36
Arnold, 21
Axelrod, Robert, 10

B

Banco Nacional, 22
Bank of Montreal, 22
Banting, Keith, 29, 30
Baril, Marcel, 27
Baring Bank, 21
Beckett, Samuel, 86
Bédard, Guy, 42
Behiels, Michael, 41
Bernd, Zila, 16, 51
Bernier, Léon, 42
Berthe, A., 20
Bhabha, Homi, 28
Bilbao, Francisco, 16
Biron, Michel, 62
Bissoondath, Neil, 31
Bombardier, 22
Borges, 93

Bourget, Monseigneur, 20
Bouchard, Gérard, 5, 7, 16, 51, 57, 60, 68, 71
Branach-Kallas, A., 15
Brochu, A., 63

C

Caccia, Fulvio, 96
Callage Neto, Roque, 46, 48
Canchola Camacho, Maria Guadalupe, 45
Caron, R. E., 18
Carvalho, Mathias, 24
Cascade, 22
Castells, Manuel, 9
Castillo Durante, Daniel, 5, 8, 26, 37, 40, 49, 73, 77, 85, 90, 97, 98
CGI, 23
Chamber of Commerce of the Province of Québec, 27
Chanady, Amaryll, 70
Cirque du Soleil, Le, 22, 36

Clinton, H., 21
Cole, Laurie, 33
Colin, Amy, 40, 49
Couillard, Marie, 22, 49, 78
Cousin, Victor, 16

D

de Nevers, Edmond, 69
de Pauw, 59
de Soto, Hernando, 15
Dessaulles, Louis-Antoine, 17
Dion, Céline, 36
Docola, Silvia, 22
Drache, Daniel, 44
Ducharme, Réjean, 62

E

Enrique López, Luis, 30

F

Faucher de St-Maurice, Narcisse, 16
Ferron, Jacques, 62
Frappier, Roger, 35

G

Garaud, Christian, 85
García Canclini, Néstor, 11, 37, 38
Geertz, Clifford, 28

Gloria Garbarini, Carmen, 30
Groulx, Lionel, 71

H

Harvey, Jean-Charles, 19
Hazelton, Hugh, 35
Hébert, Anne, 75, 76
Heidegger, M., 76
Hones, Sheila, 45
Humboldt, 59
Huston, Nancy, 8, 87, 88, 89, 90, 94

I

Imbert, Odette, 2
Imbert, Patrick, 3, 4, 5, 10, 13, 15, 22, 24, 26, 28, 35, 37, 40, 48, 64, 78, 94
Iyer, Pico, 27

K

Kadir, Djelal, 45
Katrapani, Phyllis, 26
Kerouac, Jack, 25
Klepak, Hal P., 34
Kokis, Sergio, 8, 38, 79, 80, 81, 82, 83, 85, 86, 87
Kymlicka, Will, 29, 30, 31

L

Laferrière, Dany, 8, 40, 80, 81, 85
Lamartine, 16
Lamennais, 16
Lepage, Guy A., 35
Lesemann, Frédéric, 41
Lévi-Strauss, Claude, 64
Leyda, Julia, 45
Lincoln, 48
Lipset, Seymour Martin, 39
Locke, John, 16

M

Mann, Horace, 19
Martel, Yann, 36, 94
Martin, Paul, 33
McClure, S. S., 39
Michaux, G., 62
Miron, Gaston, 76
Mondelet, Charles, 19
Monroe, 68
Montesquieu, 59
Moreno, García, 20
Morgenstern, 10
Morisset, Jean, 24
Mulroney, Brian, 33
Murat, A., 24

N

Napoleon III, 16, 21
Nardout-Lafarge, É., 62

O

Ollivier, Émile, 95
Ouellet, F., 23

P

Papineau, 23
Paquet, Gilles, 37, 38
Parent, Étienne, 20
Perkins, William, 22
Pettigrew, Pierre, 44
Poulin, Jacques, 25

R

Riel, Louis, 14, 24
Rizzo, Adriana, 36, 78
Robin, Régine, 90, 91, 92
Rockland, Michael Aaron, 20, 25
Rousseau, 16
Roy, Gabrielle, 63
Ryerson, Egerton, 19

S

Sábato, Ernesto, 77, 97
Sade, 97
Saint-Simon, 16
Samaniego, Mario, 30
Sarmiento, Domingo Faustino, 15, 19, 20, 25, 48, 77
Say, Jean-Baptiste, 16
Schwaben, Daniel, 34
Siemerling, Winfried, 96

Smith, Adam, 16
SNC Lavalin, 23
Soares de Souza, Licia, 58
Stinson, Robert, 39
Subiela, Eliseo, 35

T

Tapscott, Don, 37, 38
Tchoungui, Gisele, 34
Tocqueville, 25
Toffler, Alvin, 37
Toro, Fermin, 23, 24
Tremblay, Michel, 63
Trudeau, 28, 48

V

Van Schendel, Michel, 75
Vargas, 48
Vasconcelos, Jose, 69
Vigneault, Gilles, 74
Voltaire, 16
Von Neumann, 10

W

Washington, 21
Welnic, E., 15
Welsh, Jennifer M., 42
Wojcik, J., 15